RICKY MARTIN

RICKY MARTIN

La Vida Loca

Patricia J. Duncan

A Time Warner Company

Warner Books, Inc., 1271 Avenue of the Americas, New York, NY 10020

Visit our Web site at www.warnerbooks.com

A Time Warner Company

Printed in the United States of America

First Warner Books Printing: August 1999

10 9 8 7 6 5 4 3 2 1

ISBN: 0-446-67628-4

LC: 99-63946

Book Design: HRoberts Design

ACKNOWLEDGMENTS

Thank you to the following people:

The people at Warner Books, especially my editor, Diana Baroni, and Diane Luger, Carolyn Lechter, Anna Maria Piluso, Harvey-Jane Kowal and Bob Castillo. Special thanks also to my agent, Laura Dail, and to her assistant, Francheska Farinacci.

CONTENTS

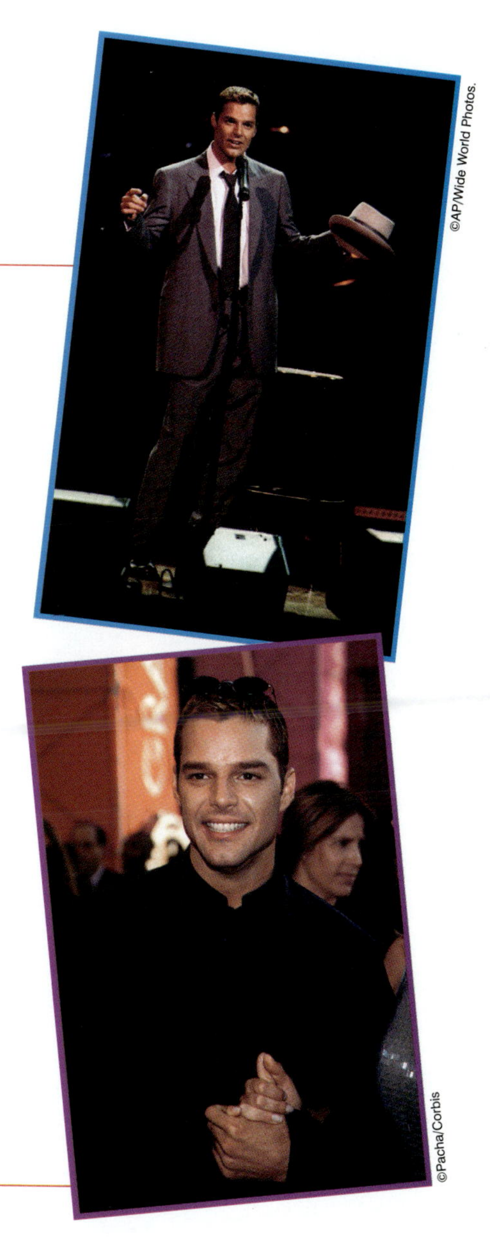
©AP/Wide World Photos.
©Pacha/Corbis

RICKY MARTIN

Ricky Martin, Madison Square Garden Concert.
©Corbis/Mitch Gerber

I

INTRODUCTION

Puerto Ricans and Latinos all over are no doubt asking themselves, Why now? What took so long? Ricky Martin, who fifteen years ago, as a member of the popular teenage pop group Menudo, had already found his way into the hearts of Latino fans everywhere, has finally served his notice on the music industry. Whether it was his electrifying, hip-gyrating performance of "La Copa de la Vida" at the 1999 Grammy Awards, or simply that the time was right, and the Anglo market was finally ready to accept Ricky Martin and his Latin pop music with its blend of diverse rhythms, Ricky Martin is impacting the North American music industry in a way that few have been able to do. He has made the jump from the Latino market to the highly difficult-to-

Ricky holds his coveted Grammy Award.

penetrate North American market smoothly and successfully. Ricky Martin is making the Latino presence in the music world known with a new energy and vitality, and he is blurring the distinction between what is exclusively Latino and what is not. While remaining fiercely loyal to his Puerto Rican roots, he is also representative of a new biculturalism.

With over 13 million albums sold worldwide, Ricky Martin and his Latin pop have filled stadiums with adoring fans throughout Latin America and Europe, as well as India, Japan, China and Australia. This 6'2" superstar knockout is now taking the U.S. market by storm, proving that Latinos can succeed outside of their own market. Voted one of *People*'s 50 most beautiful people in the world in 1999, Ricky Martin is adored by women and men of all ages, races and cultures. His appeal and talent have broken cultural and linguistic barriers. Over 2 billion people in all corners of the world watched as he sang the theme song he wrote for the World Cup games in 1998, "La Copa de la Vida," at the final game in Paris. More than 1.5 billion around the world watched his dazzling performance of the same song on the 1999 Grammy Awards show. He was the first Hispanic artist to perform in China, the world's most populated country. His impeccable appearance and good looks make him noticed wherever he goes, but his talent has made him an international superstar.

Since leaving the teenage heartthrob band Menudo over ten years ago, Ricky Martin's solo career has included roles on television soap operas in Mexico and the United States, roles on stage in Mexico and then later on Broadway, and a music career that he never once abandoned and which has earned him a Grammy Award. But Ricky is now dedicating himself fully to his music career. With his English language album he is showing the world that breaking down cultural barriers is what it is all about, and that communication, in whatever language, is the force that unites us all. Ricky Martin's development as a solo recording artist has been distinguished by his refusal to be average. He was born to be in front of an audience, and he was intent on not taking the easy road, and this meant never conforming to what the industry expected of a Latino performer.

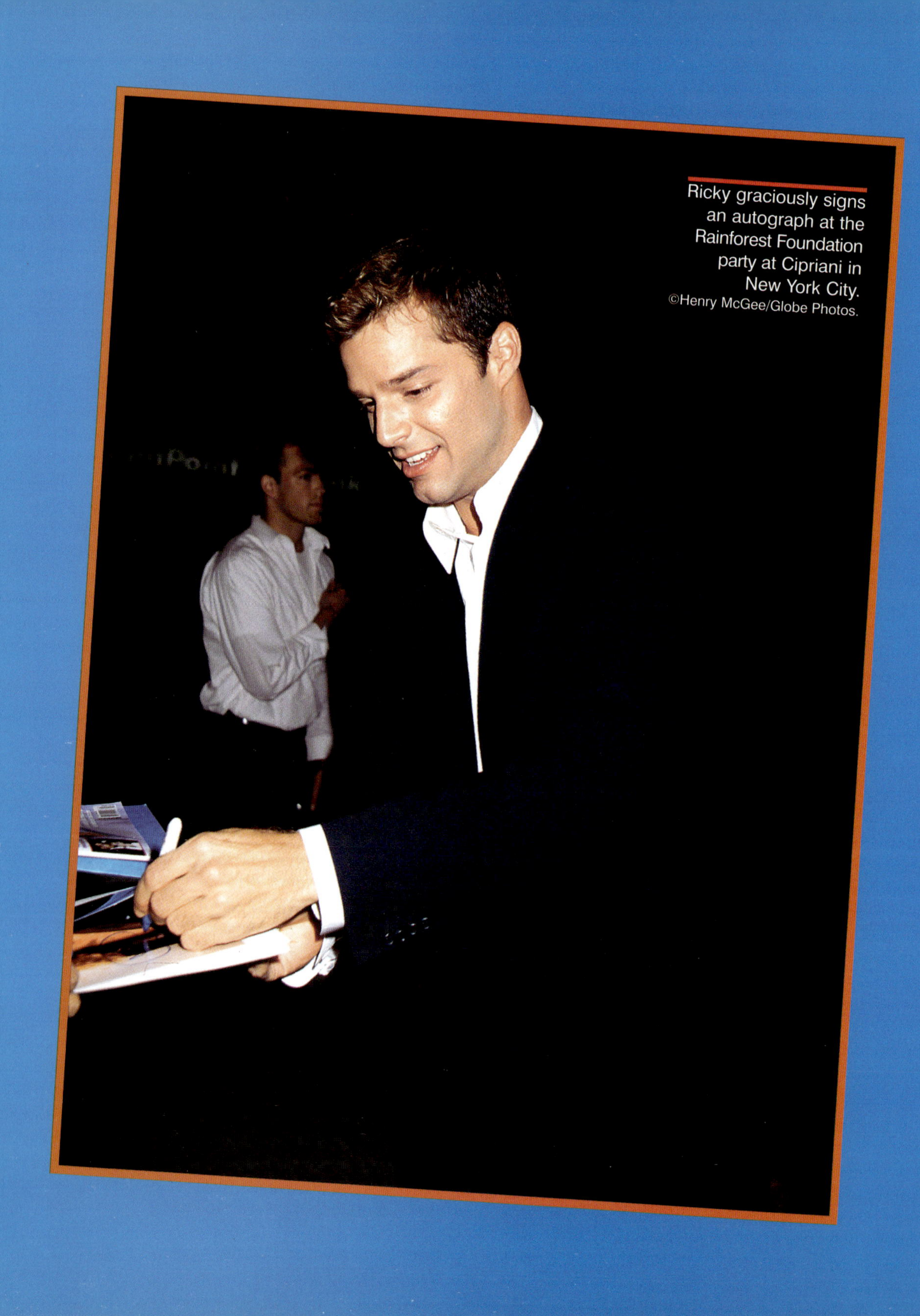

Ricky graciously signs an autograph at the Rainforest Foundation party at Cipriani in New York City.

Ricky Martin has gone from Puerto Rican superstar to superstar of the world. He has become an ambassador for Puerto Rico and for all Latin America. In reaching out to the world, whether in English or Spanish, whether in Asia or India, Ricky is bringing pride to his island nation and to all Latino people. He has brought Latin pop music to the mainstream, and he has brought his language and his culture to the world, demonstrating to all that he can remain who he is, Puerto Rican, and still achieve the heights of fame that have previously been all but unreachable for Latino artists. By excluding negative words from his vocabulary, and keeping a positive outlook throughout his career, he has shown that Latinos *can* succeed in the mainstream with their *own* music and their *own* rhythms. Ricky is opening the world's eyes to Spanish music and to the Latin pop music industry, and different cultures around the world are finding these new rhythms easy to embrace. And with his movement into the U.S. market, recording in English, he is opening the world's eyes to a new kind of star, one who transcends both linguistic and cultural barriers, a star whose "people" are the people of the world.

The repercussions of Ricky Martin's crossover into the North American market will surely play out for some time to come. The sounds of Latin pop music, once heard only on Spanish language radio stations, can now be heard on Top 40 stations around the country. By remaining steadfast and determined in his goal to dispel old myths about his country and his culture, Ricky has given the world the gift of his music. The timid but determined Puerto Rican singing sensation has quietly snuck up on the American market and successfully taken his pulsating Latin rhythms mainstream. Fans from all corners of the world, men and women of all ages, colors and cultures, are moving their bodies to its infectious beat, and there's nothing quiet about that.

Ricky Martin joined Menudo at age twelve, and here you see the joy of performing in his eyes.
©Corbis.

II

In the Beginning

Ricky Martin's climb to stardom began on a small Caribbean island where the Latin sounds and rhythms drift through the streets and permeate the souls of all who live there. Born Enrique Martin Morales on Christmas Eve, December 24, 1971, in Hato Rey, a suburb of San Juan, Puerto Rico, Ricky Martin was raised in a middle-class home, surrounded by his large family. His mother, Nereida Morales, an accountant, and his father, Enrique, a psychologist, divorced when Ricky was only two years old. But Ricky was in good hands and had no lack of family support. He had two older stepbrothers, Fernando and Angel, from his mother's previous marriage; and three younger siblings, Eric, Vanessa and Daniel, from his father's subsequent marriage. He was also surrounded by many other family members, including cousins, who lived on the island.

Named after his father Enrique but called Ricky by most (and Kiki by his mother), Ricky Martin recalls a normal, happy childhood despite his parents being divorced and not living with him under one roof. He went to school every day (Ricky attended Catholic schools), like most kids his age, and even saw having two homes where he could visit and live as a great advantage. Ricky remained close to both of his parents. "I did whatever I wanted. I lived with my mother when I wanted to be with her, and with my father in the same way. I had the same affection from both of them. Although they were no longer married, they were very good friends." Both his parents provided him with the support he needed, and he recalls his life as a young boy as quite normal.

However, his life did not remain normal for very long. Once Ricky discovered the beat of Latin music, he began to dream. His mother was instrumental in Ricky learning to appreciate the Latin sound. Like other boys his age, his brothers included, Ricky liked rock music, and listened to Boston, Cheap Trick, Journey and David Bowie, among others. But his mother gave him a musical lesson that he has not forgotten to this day. Exasperated by their choice of music, Ricky's mother took her children to a concert by the legendary Celia Cruz, a moment in Ricky's life that he feels profoundly affected him.

Ricky's penchant for performing for others also developed when he was very young. He recalls gathering all his neighbors together to do a play in the street—his first onstage appearance—with his friends. He was barely six years old when he told his father that he wanted to be in show business. His father probably did not take him too seriously, but he proved that young as he was, he knew *just* what he wanted to do with himself. He had actually already been exposed to the public as an infant, having won a baby competition. And he had shown great interest in performing when he was at school, participating in school plays and the school choir. By age eight Ricky was in front of the cameras again, having appeared in television commercials and even winning an award for a commercial in which he appeared for Carnation.

Ricky was a natural. He was comfortable in front of the camera as a baby and as a young boy, and he loved that people were watching him perform. As his parents saw Ricky's interest in performing develop during these years, they were surprisingly supportive of his goals, something for which Ricky is grateful. They enrolled him in acting and singing lessons so that he could learn even more. Ricky also recalls watching television and how this made him dream and may very well have had a strong impact on his desire to be an artist. Through television he was exposed to show business and to the rhythms and the sounds of his culture. And Ricky wanted to imitate what he was seeing and hearing, whether in his school plays or on the neighborhood streets.

While the young Ricky Martin was still a child and was pursuing his childhood dreams, he enjoyed the loving and nurturing of his family. It was this supportive environment that is no doubt responsible for the importance that Ricky places on family today. He describes his relationship with his family, then and to this day, as warm. "Family is the most important thing for me. When I feel alone on tours, I take a deep breath and think about them. I think about where I came from, where I am going and where I am." He has an excellent relationship with his mother, whom he describes as his best friend and someone with whom he can share his feelings, and she often travels with him. He adores his mother and recognizes that she spoils him, something about which he does not complain, especially when she prepares his favorite dish of rice and beans for him. She has also worked with him, as his accountant. The relationship with his father suffered a bit more in later years, due to Ricky's frenetic travel schedule and his not being able to spend as much time with him. But the two, Enrique son and Enrique father, would eventually be able to find their way back to the good relationship they had enjoyed when Ricky was a young boy.

Ricky Martin's normal, middle-class childhood started to become just a bit more exceptional when his face began to appear more and more on television, advertising various products. Ricky's dreams were indeed coming true. While other boys his age were playing outside with their friends, Ricky Martin was developing into a goal-oriented young man and realizing, as young as he was, that he wanted something very deeply. His goal was to be an entertainer. He would act on stage, appear in commercials, whatever it would take to be in the public light and to show people who he was and what he could do. He was learning perseverance, a quality that to this day characterizes the talented Puerto Rican entertainer.

Young Ricky Martin knew that he was destined for bigger and greater successes. He had been raised by a loving family who encouraged him in all his efforts, had been influenced by the power of television at home and was infected by the culture and rhythms of his people. But as a mere teenager, he was just steps away from leaving all that behind, for a period in his young life that would lead him to the stardom of which he had always dreamed.

Ricky sings his heart out.
©Corbis

The five members of Menudo, including Ricky at the bottom left, sit for a publicity shot in 1987.
©Corbis/Bettman

III

MENUDO BOUND

Almost from the moment Ricky Martin discovered the Latin pop group Menudo, he knew that he had found his destiny. A huge fan since the group's inception in 1977, when he was only six years old, Ricky was captivated by the group's singing and dancing. Ricky had already shown an interest in performing at that time, and it was then that he made a goal of one day becoming part of the teen music sensation.

At this young age, Ricky's world already included the stage. His performances in school plays and the school choir no longer seemed enough to satisfy the budding star. He wanted to perform on a greater and more visible level. He wanted exposure—lots of exposure—and he wanted that attention from around the world, as he saw it showered on the members of Menudo.

Today, Ricky Martin is very candid in reflecting upon that time in his childhood. His purpose in joining Menudo was quite clear. It was not a singing career that he craved but rather the lifestyle that the band members enjoyed and the attention they basked in. "What I wanted was to be in Menudo. I wanted to give concerts, to travel, to meet the pretty girls." Not an unusual wish for a young teenage boy whose natural ability to perform for an audience seemed to energize him rather than terrify him. Ricky Martin had set his first goal, and he would soon prove to the world that no matter how unreachable a goal may seem, determination and a belief in what you are seeking *do* make a difference.

At the time that the teenage pop group Menudo was formed in 1977, it was the first band of its kind. The idea behind the group—one that has since inspired subsequent boys' bands like the popular Backstreet Boys and New Kids on the Block—was a unique concept for the music world. Particular to Menudo, however, was that only boys of a certain age would be allowed to join and perform with the group. The target audience was young people, and so the band would be comprised of young boys who appealed to their own age group, boys and girls alike. The group members would be teenage boys from age twelve to seventeen. Any boy younger or older than those age limits would not fit the image or sound of the group and would therefore not be eligible for inclusion.

In the summer of 1978, Menudo did what no other musical group before had been able to do. They broke down the language barrier in the United States. They achieved that goal so often elusive for Spanish language performers:

Ricky singing, dancing and in costume, as the newest member of Menudo. New York, 1984.
©Corbis

The five members of Menudo are dressed up and waving. 1984.
©Globe Photos.

they *crossed over*. Their arrival in New York City caused great excitement among teenagers, Latino and non-Latino alike. The group's popularity soared from there, and they were soon being seen and heard not only live but on television specials and even in a feature film. Menudo was soon a worldwide success, with young people everywhere clamoring for tickets to their live performances.

By 1983, Menudo was breaking records for having the largest audiences in attendance at their concerts. The group, in fact, held the top three spots in the *Guinness Book of World Records* for the largest audiences ever. In Mexico City, 30,000 fans packed Azteca Stadium for three straight days to watch their idols sing and dance. With the release of their album *Evolución* in 1986, Menudo became a sensation around the world, and the following year they found themselves performing to sell-out crowds in Latin America, the United States, Japan, the Philippines and Italy. Menudo mania was spreading, and the group continued to wow their fans and produce more and more albums. Menudo's first greatest hits album entitled *La Colección* hit stores in April 1990. It was so well received by fans that they put out yet another greatest hits album that same year, entitled *Menudo la Década*.

For almost sixteen years the Latin teenage pop group maintained the same image and continued to add new fans to their already overwhelming following. But in 1993, the group's music and image took a departure from the well-known and loved clean-cut image and sound that had always characterized Menudo. The sound that had made them famous was now replaced by the sound of rap and hip-hop. Menudo suffered a decline during this period, but has since made a comeback, with all new members, and is recouping its popularity of old and once again winning fans and followers around the world.

Ricky Martin's patience was tested as he pursued his goal of joining the hot teen band that was enjoying some of its best years. The group adhered strictly to the policy of selecting only boys of a certain age that would best maintain the sound and image of that musical phenomenon known as Menudo. Ricky auditioned before he had reached the age of twelve, and he was, therefore, not chosen. Despite his young age, the manager of Menudo at that time, Edgardo Díaz, recognized Ricky's natural talent, saying that "we saw that he had a magical quality." Ricky did not give up, and in 1984, at age twelve, he performed yet another audition. He shone again, and he was chosen to become the next member of Menudo. Ricky looks back on that life-changing moment with genuine awe. He told *People en Español* in May 1999, "One day I was riding my bicycle in the park and the next I was on stage singing in front of 200,000 people." Just one day after his parents had

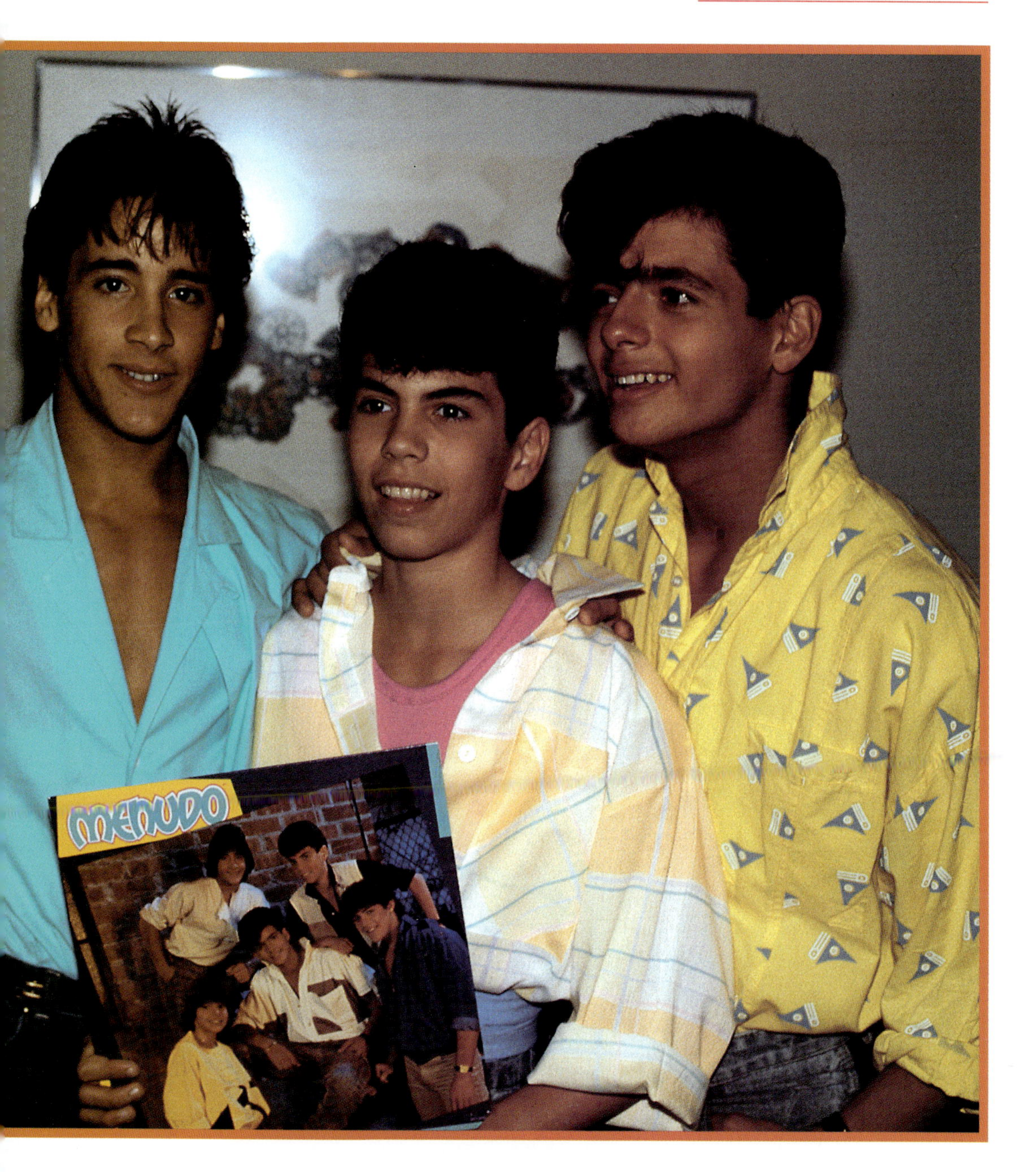

Ricky with three other members of Menudo, holding copies of their new album. 1985.
©Corbis

Ricky was happy to sign autographs for two enthusiastic fans.
©Corbis

signed the contract, the young Ricky left on a plane bound for Orlando, Florida, to film an advertisement for the group. At the young age of twelve, Ricky Martin had made a choice that would change the course of his life forever.

By joining the third generation of the ever-changing group that was Menudo, Ricky Martin was fulfilling a dream and opening the door to many others. The five years that Ricky would spend with the group would help develop him as a performer. They were filled with the excitement, the travel to faraway lands, and the attention from adoring girls that he had sought. But those years were also difficult for Ricky, a teenager who had to leave his family behind and grow up quickly and on his own. His parents were taken aback by Ricky's ability to leave them and his school life behind. It was his excitement for what was now within reach that made this step possible for Ricky. "I was so enthusiastic about being part of the group that even my parents were surprised about how easily I could distance myself from them. It seemed unreal to them that a child who was so mild-mannered, and loved being home so much, could leave without any regrets." His ambition ran deep, though, and he embarked on this stage of his life with enthusiasm and without looking back.

The routine of Menudo, which consisted of many months on the road, tireless rehearsing, and three hours of tutoring each day, soon became Ricky Martin's daily reality. He quickly learned the meaning of discipline, a discipline that many former Menudo members would later look back upon and characterize as abusive. The nonstop rehearsing, tours, recording and traveling were difficult for all of the group members, and despite Ricky's carefree nature, he was no exception. All of the visible flattery and excitement was

complemented by agonizing days and an absence of the freedom that other teenage boys could enjoy.

Ricky reflects on that thrilling yet trying period, one which he even characterizes as "suffocating," and is able to be very forgiving in light of the fact that professionally he gained much more than he lost from his experience as a member of Menudo. He was forced to develop a sense of self-sufficiency and independence. He no longer had his mother to pack his suitcase or prepare his favorite foods for him. He had to adjust to discipline and strict codes of behavior—something that he was not accustomed to. But this change in routine was extremely valuable for Ricky, who in continuing to pursue his artistic career after leaving Menudo would benefit enormously from the discipline that had been forced upon him at such an early age. He is now able to credit those tough years of strict rules with giving him training and a focus that contributed a great deal to his future professional career. He may have missed the traditional high school experience, but he received a schooling that proved invaluable in helping him achieve worldwide success as a solo performer.

But while Ricky Martin was off traveling and winning new fans in countries around the world, his relationship with his family was suffering. The lengthy trips—sometimes three months on the road at a time—put a strain on his relationship with both parents. While anticipating Ricky's return before a break for the group,

Most of Menudo hanging out on a balcony. New York City, 1985.
©Corbis

his divorced parents would argue over with whom Ricky would stay while he was back home in Puerto Rico. They put Ricky himself in the awkward position of having to choose with whom he wanted to stay. That upsetting, painfully awkward aspect of his time away from the group affected Ricky profoundly. His relationship with his mother survived this fragile period, but his relationship with his father fell apart, something that Ricky's father recalls as "sad and very painful." This rift in their relationship lasted for eight years, until the distance that had been created between them simply became too much to bear. Ricky recalls always being in a bad mood and eventually realizing that in order to save himself he had to restore his relationship with his father. Since their reconciliation, he has not been able to hold a grudge against anyone. "And from that point on," he says, "my life has been wonderful."

Ricky Martin quickly went from being too young to being too old. In 1989, at the age of seventeen, he had outgrown the teen group and was rotated out. The difficult and challenging Menudo years had given Ricky great confidence, and he felt well prepared to face the world and the next stage in his life, whatever that held. "I gave Menudo all I had, and when I felt it was the moment to part with them, I left completely convinced that I was ready for another stage of both my career and my life." But he was tired and he needed a break. He was also undecided about which direction to take with respect to his career. His first decision was an easy one—return to Puerto Rico and finish high school.

With his education completed, he decided to disconnect for a while—take some time off and catch his breath after the five intense and demanding years that he had lived. He chose to do his reflecting in New York City, where he spent a much needed six-month break, until he was ready to take that next great step in his life.

Ricky Martin owes a great deal to his experience as a teen idol and member of the first Latin pop group to break down cultural and linguistic barriers. While his life as a teen star, from July 10, 1984, to July 10, 1989, was characterized by a strict regimen, military-style discipline and an atmosphere that he calls suffocating, he recognizes the importance of the experience and is able to see how what he endured has helped him move forward in his career. He gave his all to the group, but in return he left with a preparation and maturity that gave him the sense that he could continue with his career—with the confidence and the focus that he so needed in order to be successful.

Joining Menudo and becoming a teen idol and worldwide pop star were only the beginning for Ricky Martin. His hard work and the focus that had been instilled in him would soon be put to an even greater use as he explored his artistic talents alone, without his former group members. His desire to perform and to win fans and admirers was still very much alive, only it would now be channeled in a different direction.

Ricky Martin. 1995, L.A.

IV

Flying Solo

With Menudo now just a memory and his period of reflection in New York City winding down, Ricky Martin was ready to embark on the next stage of his professional career, a stage that he would initiate by pursuing his second passion, acting. While Ricky had not forgotten what would prove to be his true destiny, singing, he felt an urge to explore other areas. And so he set off in search of a new kind of stardom.

Ricky traveled from New York City to Mexico, where he would remain for three years, developing his talents as both an actor and a singer. He dedicated his first year there to establishing himself as an actor, without, however, ever abandoning his love for singing. Ricky began his career in

Ricky was on top of Los Angeles in 1995.

Mexico by acting in musical plays. In mid-September 1990, he landed a role in the theater production *Las Zapatillas Rojas* and his successful performance in this role led to his next opportunity, a leading role in the play *Mi Mamá Ama el Rock* (Mom Loves Rock). Ricky's talent as an actor was immediately recognized and rewarded. His role in this play won him the reputable Eres award.

But Ricky's luckiest break as an actor came when he was offered a role on the well-known Mexican soap opera *Alcanzar una Estrella* (To Reach a Star). Like the parts that he had played on stage, in his role as Pablo Ricky was cast as a musician and a singer. He played this role for almost two years, and sang the theme song for the series. The series was so popular that it was spun off into a movie entitled *Más que Alcanzar una Estrella*. His performance in this, his first motion picture film, made the Mexican motion picture industry sit up and take notice. He was awarded the prestigious "El Heraldo" award, which is the Mexican equivalent of an Academy Award. The series *Alcanzar una Estrella* also provided Ricky the opportunity to record an ensemble-type album entitled *Muñecos de Papel*. Each star in the series sang a song on the album. So while Ricky Martin was testing the waters in the field of acting, he continued to develop as a singer, independent of Menudo. After expanding his artistic talents in theater, film and television, Ricky was ready for his next venture, finding his way back to his music.

In 1991 Ricky signed with Sony Discos in Mexico and released his first solo album. The album, entitled simply *Ricky Martin*, was compelling proof that Ricky would, indeed, be able to succeed as a solo artist. He wrote the album along with another former Menudo member, Robi

Rosa, who would continue to play an important role in Ricky's future musical endeavors. *Ricky Martin* turned out to be a success in Latin America, and it went platinum in many countries. While it did not launch his career as a singing sensation overnight, it did push him one step closer to reaching the maturity and versatility that come through in his later albums.

Ricky continued to reach out to the public through his music with his next album, released just two years later. Entitled *Me Amarás*, it showed that Ricky Martin had enormous possibilities to make it in the international music scene. Produced by Juan Carlos Calderon, this album put Ricky at the top of the Latin music charts for the first time as a solo artist, and it also earned him *Billboard*'s award for Best New Latin Artist at the publication's 1993 music awards. Ricky Martin, the solo performer, had now reached star status in Latin America.

While singing seemed to be Ricky's natural destiny, he was not yet ready to put his acting career to the side. In January 1994, Ricky Martin made a move that would propel his career forward in a way he had yet to experience. The success that he had achieved in Mexico and in Latin America had not gone entirely undetected by the American television industry. It wasn't long before ABC offered Ricky a role on the popular long-running daytime soap opera *General Hospital*. The exposure that this role would give Ricky Martin—one hour a day every day in front of a North American audience—would lead to numerous opportunities.

On *General Hospital*, Ricky's role again involved his true passion, singing. His character, Miguel Morez, was a former pop star from Puerto Rico who worked as a bar-

Ricky took a date to the 1994 Daytime Emmy Awards. His part in the ABC soap opera *General Hospital* was his first North American television role.

Ricky wore a tux to the 22nd Annual Daytime Emmy Awards in 1995.
©Jonathan Green/Globe Photos

tender and added heat and sex appeal to the series. He got to showcase his musical talent in his role as Miguel, during recording sessions and live performances. The impact that this career move had on Ricky's future was significant, as it made him extremely popular with the U.S. audience, and he was now talked about on many programs such as *Entertainment Tonight* and *Hard Copy*. And Ricky knows that he owes a lot to the exposure from the daytime series. "Who could complain about having spent an hour a day for three years on American television? To introduce myself and become known, it was good." He had successfully crossed the border and was making a name for himself outside of the Latino community.

Ricky's breakthrough appearance on *General Hospital* led to another career first—an appearance in a hit Broadway musical. In June 1996, Ricky returned to New York to perform in the musical adaptation of Victor Hugo's classic *Les Misérables*. He was offered the part by executive producer Richard-Jay Alexander, who had read an interview given by Martin in which he stated that he needed to act on Broadway before he died. After reading that interview, Alexander called Ricky and met with him. After hearing Ricky's singing range, he offered him the part. *Les Misérables* was one of Broadway's hottest tickets, and it was a work that demanded excellent singing ability. Ricky proved to be the perfect choice for Marius, the idealistic young university student in Paris at the time of the French Revolution. It is a romantic role which includes several songs—a perfect fit for the tall, handsome recording artist.

Ricky had to take on more than just the challenge of playing his first role on Broadway. In addition to his primary character role as Marius, he had to play three other roles.

During his *General Hospital* days, long hair and denim were Ricky's style.
©Robert Milazzo/Corbis

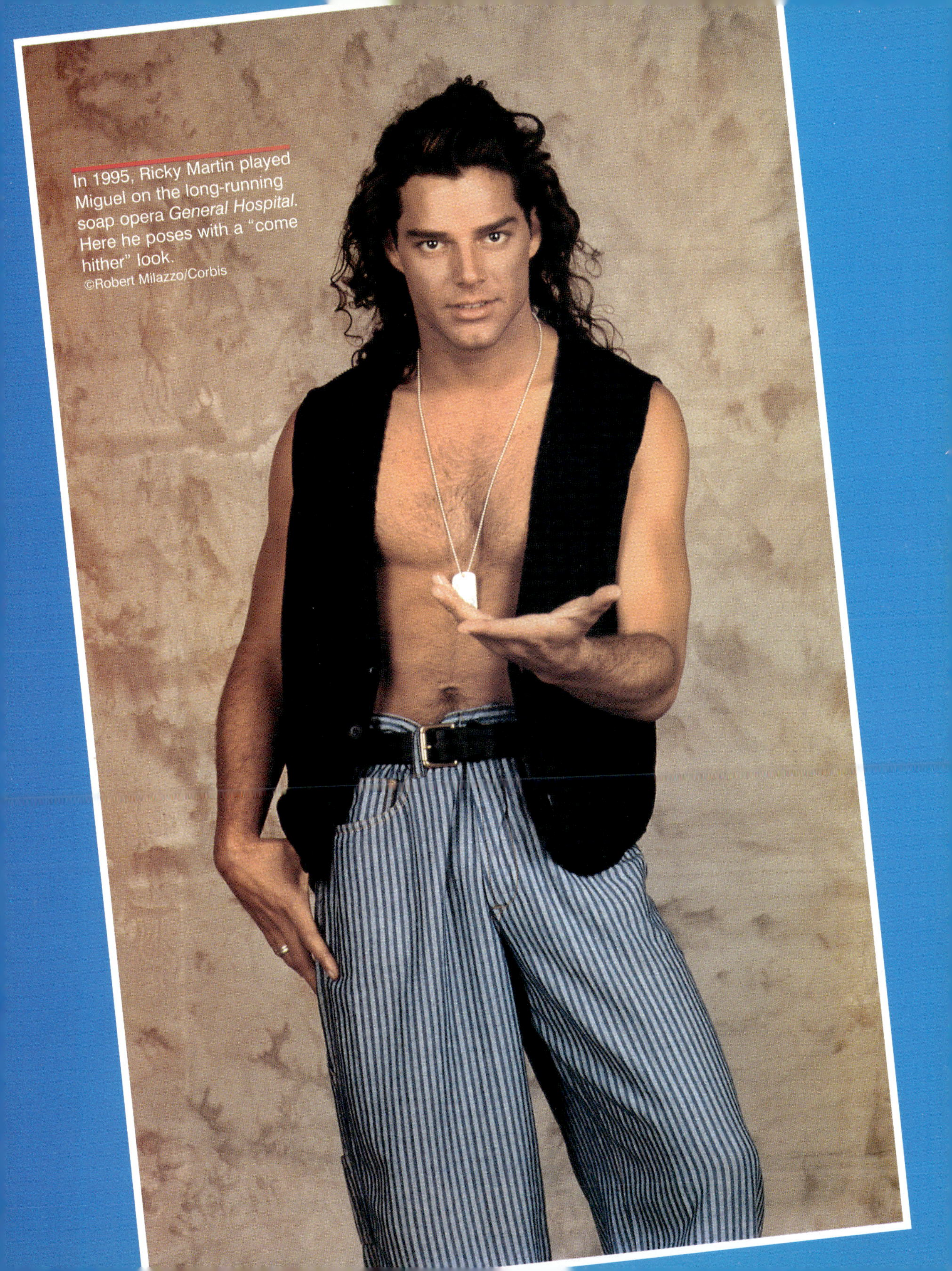

In 1995, Ricky Martin played Miguel on the long-running soap opera *General Hospital*. Here he poses with a "come hither" look.
©Robert Milazzo/Corbis

In June 1996 Ricky made his Broadway debut as Marius in the musical adaptation of Victor Hugo's *Les Misérables.*
©Walter Weissman/ Globe Photos

Before Marius even appears on stage, Ricky portrayed a convict, a farmer and a policeman. Ricky admits being scared to death by his Broadway debut. On opening night he performed to a sold-out house, which included his grandmother who had flown up from Puerto Rico to be there. "Every single scene, from beginning to end, I was just dying because the entire theater world was sitting there watching me. Thank God everyone said to me afterward, 'Oh, you looked so comfortable up there' because I certainly didn't feel it." His ability to conquer so many roles is that much more impressive considering that he had only ten days to learn his lines! His hectic touring schedule to promote an album whisked him off to Spain after only six days of rehearsal on *Les Misérables.* When he returned, he had four more days before his opening. To make matters worse, Ricky came down with a case of laryngitis upon his return from Spain, which was no doubt due to the fatigue and stress caused by the long flights and his long rehearsal hours. When he finally did hit the stage on opening night, however, Ricky was ready to conquer the untested waters of Broadway. He told *Soap Opera Magazine,* "I felt my adrenaline pumping because the audience that goes to my concerts is already convinced [of my talent], but in the theater I still have to convince them. It was a real challenge."

Ricky Martin subsequently was given yet another opportunity to dabble in unknown territory. He was offered a

Ricky took a date to the Fire & Ice Ball in 1994
©Lisa Rose/Globe Photos

Ricky Martin added fresh sex appeal to *General Hospital*.
©Corbis/Mitch Gerber.

role in Disney's animated Spanish language version of *Hercules*. Ricky recalls this opportunity as being just as challenging as his other endeavors, but for very different reasons. The challenge, in this case, was working with an audience comprised of children, which he calls "the toughest audience there could ever be." His preparation was also intense, even though it was only his voice that was used for this part. He may not have been physically tired, but he surely must have been mentally exhausted. Yet Ricky is always dedicated to the project at hand, and as with his other experiences in the world of acting, he took his Disney role seriously and responsibly.

Ricky Martin had proven to the world that he could and should be taken seriously as an actor, both on television and on stage. But his first passion was always his singing, and while he went on to explore new frontiers as an actor, he continued recording his music and reaching out to more and more people.

Ricky Martin achieved his first truly international success with the 1995 release of his third album, *A Medio Vivir*. A hit first in America and Europe, it was soon being played all over the world. This album shows Ricky Martin for the first time as a well-rounded, wide-ranging artist, a performer who could now be accepted and lauded on an international level. Produced by Ian Blake and KC Porter (who also produced for superstars like Bon Jovi, Boyz II Men, Richard Marx and Patti LaBelle), this was clearly his highest quality recording ever, an album that combines rock, pop and Latin rhythms. It sold over 600,000 copies in the first six months, and went gold on October 27, 1997. With his third album, Ricky Martin secured his position as an international singing sensation. It was the beginning of a new direction in his musical career. Ever-present on the

album are the traditional Latin rhythms that we recognize from his previous recordings, but new are the more contemporary musical trends. These components, combined with an increased maturity, a refined talent and his always captivating charm, make this album a true departure from his other solo efforts.

The track from *A Medio Vivir* that undoubtedly catapulted Ricky Martin to international fame was "Maria." This single impacted the world and soared to the top of music charts, becoming the number one song in America and Europe. It was Sony Music's number two selling single in Europe in the summer of 1996. The infectious rhythm and beat of *"Uno, dos, tres, un pasito pa'lante Maria . . ."* won hearts around the world, as the song's popularity extended even to Asia, where this Puerto Rican charmer was winning even more admirers. The popularity of "Maria" was widespread in Brazil, where it was adopted as the theme song for the Brazilian soap opera *Salsa y Merengue.*

A Medio Vivir and the hit single "Maria" had opened the world's eyes to Ricky Martin. He was wowing audiences, male and female, all over the world with his seductive moves and that voice that was so easy to become enamored with. He was now entirely dedicated to his singing career, determined to push on and distinguish himself even further from other performers, Latino and non-Latino alike.

With just three solo albums on the market, Ricky Martin had established himself as a complete performer, a mature artist with an electrifying act. His music had

In 1995 Ricky Martin squired a lovely date out on the town.
©Corbis/Mitch Gerber

impacted almost every region of the world. He continued to sing in his native Spanish language and he continued to include and experiment with the many different Latin rhythms and sounds, but he was also making inroads into the mainstream music industry and the mainstream audience with the sounds, rhythms and language that were his culture. And this, for Ricky Martin, was what it was all about. He insisted to *Entertainment Weekly*, "It's all about breaking stereotypes. For me, the fact that people think Puerto Rico is *Scarface*, that we ride donkeys to school—that has to change." Through his music and his spectacular live performances, Ricky Martin was doing his part to reverse these cultural misconceptions.

By this turning point in his musical career, Ricky had a clear philosophy of what he intended with his style of music and how he hoped people would react to it. "I want them to feel free, liberated. I want them to be who they are with my music." He sees it as a daily challenge to produce quality material, not merely material that may make him a commercial success. He constantly strives to touch people's hearts through his songs, by singing straight from *his* heart, and he feels that he can achieve this regardless of race, culture or language. While he no doubt knows that he will never be able to please or touch everyone, he *did* succeed in getting people from around the world up and dancing to the contagious beat of "Maria," many of whom could not understand the singer's Spanish lyrics. But Ricky Martin was beginning to prove that music could go beyond one's cultural and linguistic borders and limitations. He could be who he was, show the world that the music of Puerto Rico and Latin America could also be world music.

Ricky's work was far from over, however. He was

on the verge of even greater notoriety and fame, and was about to break records that not even he could have foreseen. He had reached an important mark with his third album, *A Medio Vivir*, but it would be his fourth album that would exceed everyone's expectations, perhaps even his own. It would proclaim to the world that he, Ricky Martin, was here to stay.

Ricky Martin performs in Europe, 1998.

VUELVE

Ricky had always strived to make sure that he would never be considered mediocre, "just one more," and if he wanted to stay on the top and in the hearts and ears of people around the world, he needed to stay focused and continue to reestablish and reaffirm his star status. What's more, Ricky would make sure that he continued to evolve as an artist, so that his sound would not be repetitive and therefore cease to capture audiences.

In 1998, after more than two years of hard work, what would be Ricky Martin's most diverse, not to mention most successful, album to date was finally released, to the delight of his expectant fans. Work on *Vuelve* began during the Christmas holidays in 1996, when Ricky was in Puerto Rico along with his good friend Robi Rosa and KC Porter, the producers of his previous album, *A Medio Vivir.* Instead of taking it easy, Ricky shut himself up in a recording studio with Rosa, and together they began to collaborate on his next album. That brainstorming session produced the track that they first called "Le, lo, lai," but which is now entitled "Lola, Lola." The remainder of the songs were recorded in various countries, and Ricky recalls it as a difficult endeavor that took them two years of organizing, coordinating and traveling. They had to stop in the middle of a tour, fly the production team to Spain to record one number, then head north to France, to record one more. The journey later took Ricky to Brazil during Carnival, and it was there that he decided to incorporate the Brazilian rhythms that greatly influenced *Vuelve*. It was an intense effort but one which certainly paid off for Ricky, who prides himself on doing things, not perfectly, since, as he believes, only God can do that, but doing them well.

Ricky was aware that after the success of his first three albums, he had to continue to be innovative so as not to bore the public. He respects his listeners, and therefore wants always to surprise them, challenge them. "We have to do anything to keep music alive. I am presenting myself as who I am, a fusion." Ricky Martin is indeed a fusion of rhythms. Hailing from an island that is a combination of three cultures—Spanish, African and Indian—Ricky Martin demonstrated on this album more than any other his penchant for mixing rhythms.

This new mixture of sounds showed a Ricky Martin who has evolved in his music. By adopting sounds from many different continents and incorporating them into

In February of 1997, Ricky danced on top of a Carnival float during a parade in Rio de Janeiro, Brazil.
©AP Photo/Diego Giudice

Ricky at a European concert, 1998.
©SIN/EYECONTACT/Corbis

songs that still showcase his sexy voice and style, Martin gained new fans and increased the faith of old ones. But while expanding his scope to include new rhythms, Ricky Martin makes sure to not abandon the base of all his music—essentially Puerto Rican. "I don't want to change that, not even for the next album I am working on." Martin does not want to compromise his style for anything. "I don't want to hide behind any kind of mask," he says, and that is exactly what fans have responded so well to—his honesty and candor on stage, and his "what you see is what you get" attitude.

The difference between *Vuelve* and any of his previous albums is detected immediately. In this album, Martin emerges as a fully matured artist, reflecting his many years of experience in his songs. The album has a fresh approach, and the talents that the world had already seen and heard are further expanded upon. The diversity of Latin rhythms and the sexy Latino style have come together skillfully and successfully.

Also different for Ricky Martin are the ballads on this album. The title track, "Vuelve," with sounds that are pure and new, is a beautiful song whose inspiration comes from the Venezuelan composer Franco de Vita. Other songs, such as "Por Arriba, por Abajo" and "La Bomba," combine rhythms such as salsa and rumba with rock, jazz or pop, producing a unique sound without sacrificing the true nature of the song. "Lola, Lola"

Europe belonged to Ricky Martin in the summer of 1998. Crowds packed the square in front of the Hotel de Ville in Paris.
©Corbis/Owen Franken

is what Ricky describes as "my people, it is the Puerto Rican lament, the lament of a trumpet." Two songs that seem to expose a more intimate side of Ricky Martin are "Perdido sin Ti" and "Corazonado," both of which rely on nostalgia to convey emotion. The album also includes "No Importa la Distancia," the song that Ricky sang in the Spanish language version of Disney's *Hercules*.

Astonishing is Ricky Martin's ability to honestly express such a diversity of emotions on this album. The wide range of rhythms that he is able to so adeptly fuse together in each song is credit to his growth and maturity as a singer. *Vuelve* is a romantic album, much like its creator—romantic and dedicated to his music.

The success of Ricky Martin's *Vuelve* had taken his career to new heights as well as to new regions. *Vuelve* reached the gold mark on July 7, 1998, and it has sold over 6 million copies to date, a figure that may very well go much higher given the new life it seems to be enjoying since the February

1999 Grammy Awards. The album has gone platinum in the U.S., outselling recent releases by old-timers Van Halen and Phil Collins.

Vuelve was also Ricky's first album to celebrate such astonishing success in Asia. From Singapore to Japan to China, where Ricky Martin became the first Hispanic artist ever to perform, *Vuelve* proved to be a hit. Ricky Martin had reached the Asian people with the contagious rhythms of Latino music, sung, of course, in his native language, Spanish. *Vuelve* conquered not only Asia but also broke records in Turkey and filled stadiums with fans in Brazil and all over Europe. Even Australia and India had caught Ricky Martin fever.

Impossible to overlook and fundamental to the worldwide success of Ricky's fourth album is the hit track "La Copa de la Vida" (The Cup of Life). This is perhaps the song that introduced much of the world to Ricky and led them to discover his album *Vuelve*. "La Copa de la Vida," which was written as the official theme song for the World Cup in France in 1998, was sung by Ricky Martin at the final World Cup match in Paris on July 12, 1998. That day he had a television audience of more than one and a half billion people worldwide watching him.

Ricky performed the theme song for the 1998 World Cup, "La Copa de la Vida," at the final match in Paris.
©Corbis/Owen Franken

Ricky performing "La Copa de la Vida" during the 41st Annual Grammy Awards at the Shrine Auditorium in Los Angeles.
©AP/Wide World Photos.

On February 24, 1999, Ricky Martin won his first Grammy Award.
©Pacha/Corbis

Ricky owed this opportunity, more than likely, to the success of his hit song "Maria" in Europe. He was contacted by the English organizers of the World Cup, who told him that they liked his sound and that they wanted him to write a song with a similar feeling for the World Cup the next summer—one that contained Latin, African and Caribbean rhythms. The song was recorded in Spanish and English and was written by Robi Rosa and Desmond Child, two old friends and collaborators of Ricky's who knew him well enough to know what kind of song he would want to sing. The clearly Brazilian tone of "La Copa de la Vida" is filled with optimism and energy, so it is not surprising that it was the number one single in more than thirty countries.

Even though soccer is not an enormously popular sport in Puerto Rico, Ricky Martin had spent much time in Brazil, Mexico and Argentina, and there he witnessed first-hand the passion that fans have for the sport. It was an honor for him to be asked to participate in the World Cup in such a way, and he enjoyed the unique experience of being able to combine his music with sports. Although he admits being a pitiful soccer player, he loves everything to do with the sporting world in general. And in this case, he particularly liked the opportunity it gave him to spread his music around the globe. "The nicest thing was to be able to combine music with sports, to be able to break barriers." With "La Copa de la Vida" Ricky was able to reach an audience that he might not have been able to otherwise.

It was not only Ricky Martin's performance and the television broadcast of "La Copa de la Vida," however, that spread Martin's face and songs to places where he and his music had yet to make an impact. As a member of Menudo, Ricky Martin had received two Grammy Award nominations. But at the age of twenty-seven, the Grammy nomination he received for Best Latin Performance for his album *Vuelve* was his first solo nomination and it would prove to be an event that would set the stage for the next and biggest move in his career.

Martin was also chosen to perform his song "La Copa de la Vida" live on the Grammy broadcast, which aired February 24, 1999. He would be joining the likes of such mainstream superstars as Celine Dion, Whitney Houston, Madonna, Mariah Carey and Will Smith, who would also be participating in the event. Ricky was, understandably, thrilled at the opportunity to interpret his song, represent Latin pop and promote the Hispanic culture to the Grammy audience around the world. He was also thrilled to be able to display his talent before what he considered to be one of the toughest audiences for a singer—an audience made up of his colleagues. "I was more excited when I learned I'd be performing than when I was nominated. It was the most difficult audience I've ever been in front of! Sting! Madonna! Pavarotti! To get the acceptance of your peers really means a lot." This was an important step for Ricky personally and for Latin pop music. The president and CEO of the Recording Academy, Michael Greene, said of Martin, "As both an actor and a performer, he brings a special energy to the show. We are also committed to represent more Latin music in our future endeavors." The Recording Academy is also in the process of developing a framework for the first Latin Grammy Awards. So with Ricky Martin's nomination and slated performance on the awards show, Americans who had somehow not caught wind of this sensual singing star were given yet one more chance.

On February 24, 1999, Ricky Martin brought the house (and a large part of the billion and a half television

Ricky won two awards at the 1999 *Billboard* Latin Music Awards ceremony in Miami Beach. Here, he answers questions at a news conference backstage.

viewers in 195 countries, no doubt) to their feet with his electrifying performance of "La Copa de la Vida" at the music industry's most prestigious awards ceremony, the 41st Annual Grammy Awards, held at Los Angeles's Shrine Auditorium. Not only did Ricky's performance bring the audience to their feet, but he brought Latin pop into many homes that had never heard such rhythms before. In his tight-fitting pants and with his undeniable sex appeal, this Latin pop sensation blew the audience away with his performance, leaving them cheering for more.

After seeing him perform "La Copa de la Vida" live on the Grammys, fans around the country rushed out to stores to buy Ricky Martin's albums, most noticeably *Vuelve,* which includes the hit he performed on the awards show. This newfound frenzy in areas unknown to Ricky (and where Ricky had been previously unknown) woke the music industry up, along with everyone who had somehow managed to miss the World Cup games, *General Hospital*, the fever of "Maria," and all the other Ricky Martin accomplishments.

The 41st Annual Grammy Awards were hosted by Rosie O'Donnell, who summarized perfectly what many viewers who did not know about Ricky Martin must have been thinking as they watched him take the breath out of an unsuspecting crowd. O'Donnell stated, "I never heard of him before tonight, but I'm enjoying him so-o-o much." Rosie O'Donnell's approval and endorsement of Ricky Martin showed he had taken a giant step forward in the eyes of those who were just now discovering him. He had officially entered the mainstream and was now poised to solidify his appeal in a way that only sensations like Julio Iglesias and Gloria Estefan had been able to do.

Ricky's performance at the Grammy Awards ceremony also won him new respect among his peers, not to mention new fans. Those that he had been so anxious and nervous to perform in front of made clear to him that he now belonged to "their" world. After his performance, opera-world great Luciano Pavarotti invited him to one of his concerts. Madonna, too, was taken by the sexy Latino star, and expressed her interest in singing a duet with him, an offer that Ricky Martin did not hesitate to accept.

Ricky Martin's album *Vuelve* won the Grammy Award for the Best Latin Pop Performance, and also took home the award for Best Pop Album at the 1998 *Billboard* Latin Music Awards held in Miami, Florida, in April 1999.

Sales of this album have taken off again with this newfound fame and exposure. By breaking into the mainstream, dazzling his audience on a non-Latino awards show, Ricky Martin has impacted the music world. With his new rhythms—not so new to many—and his unique combination of talent, drive, poise and charm, not to mention sex appeal, Martin has truly become an international superstar.

While Ricky's Grammy Award could be seen as the end of a long journey in which he had been struggling for general acceptance of his music and attempting to break down stereotypes about Latin music and Latin pop stars, this achievement actually marked the beginning of yet another great challenge in Ricky Martin's singing career. His manager defined that greater challenge as "world reaffirmation of his success."

Ricky Martin is getting ready to make the boldest move of his career yet—one that, if successful, will distinguish him for all time from most pop singers and secure his place not only as one of the greatest champions of Latin music in the world but also as a great international superstar who has transcended both cultural and linguistic barriers.

Ricky performed in New Delhi in December 1998.
©AP Photo/Saurabh Das.

VI

Crossing Over

Ricky Martin has always believed that the feelings and emotions he expresses in his music are universal. It is this belief that has instilled in him the drive to succeed in all markets, not just the Latino market. If his music could touch the souls of Latinos around the world, he did not see why he could not reach an even greater populace with the same catchy rhythms and sexy lyrics that had made him the much adored superstar among the Spanish speaking world. Ricky had already proven that singing his songs in Spanish did not have to limit his success: he proved this most emphatically in Asia, a notoriously difficult market for any foreign singer to penetrate, especially a Latino. But Ricky had people in Japan, China and

At Tower Records in West Hollywood Ricky shows off his single "La Vida Loca."
©Lisa Rose/Globe Photos.

Singapore dancing to the Latino beat of his music. These rhythms needed no translation. They, too, like the emotions Ricky was conveying through his lyrics, were universal.

For Ricky Martin it was a logical move to take his ability to touch people to a higher level. He had already proven that he could reach people around the world—people who could not understand what he was singing about—with the infectious beat of the many Latin rhythms he combines on his albums. He was now poised to make the most daring move of his career. He was ready to attempt to cross over into the U.S. market, and this time he would sing to that market in their own language. This had always been part of Ricky's plan. "It was something that I always wanted to do when I started my music career in Latin America. I said that someday, somehow, I would sing in different languages. I started with Portuguese. I did a French version of one of my songs . . . so why not English? The goal is to communicate and grow." And Ricky has witnessed the success that one of his idols, Julio Iglesias, has had in attacking another market by reaching them in their language.

Ricky knew that at some point in his career he would be ready, as would the English speaking world, to make a recording in English. He was, as with everything he has done in his career, careful not to rush this move, which would be one that could expand his popularity or, possibly, fall on an indifferent public and negatively impact his career. He wanted to be completely content with what he would be releasing into the U.S. market and be convinced that the world was ready for it. "I want to listen to my music in thirty years and say 'Great album!' The time for this album is now, not because I'm ready now and I wasn't before, but because now the music is ready."

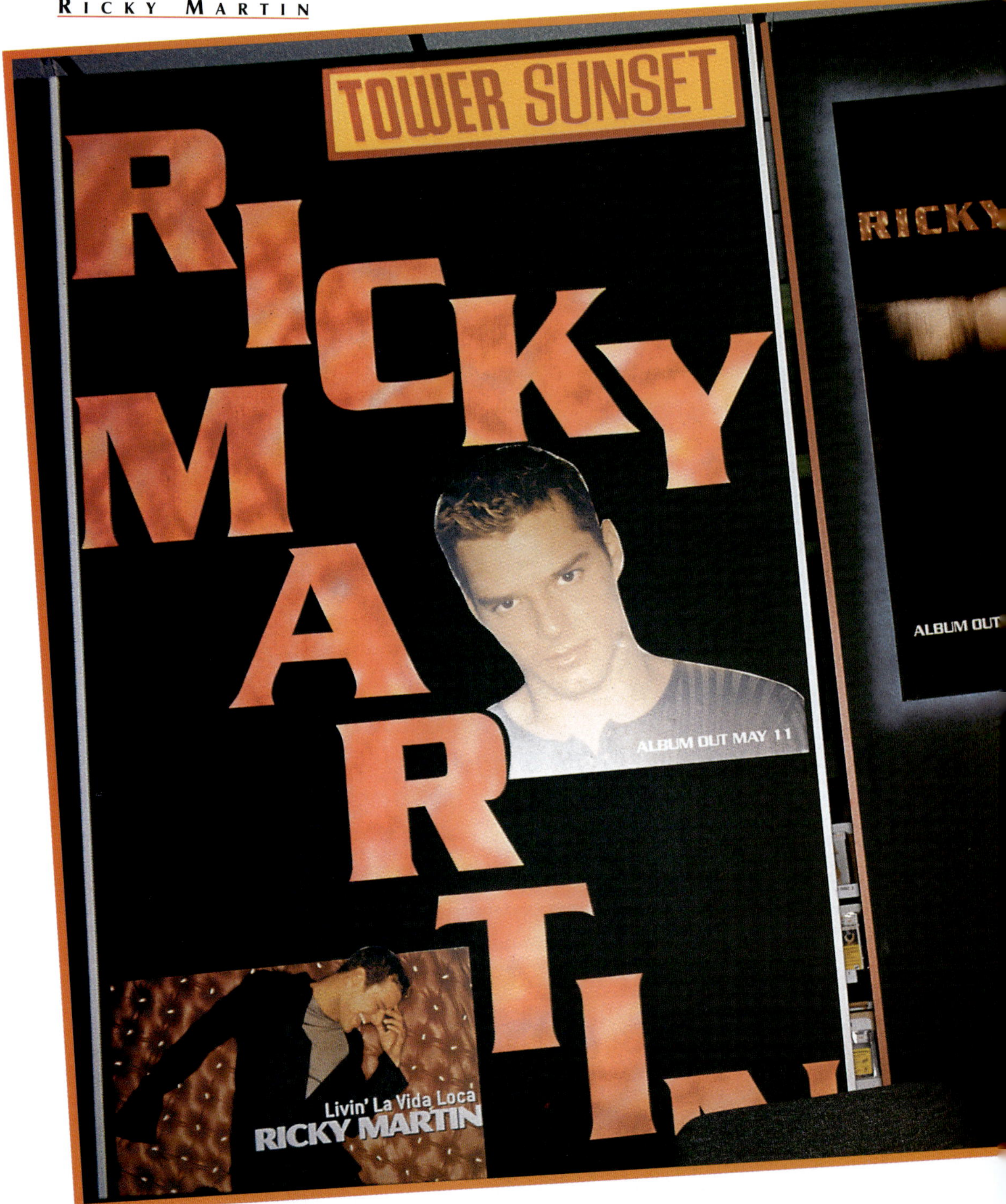
TOWER SUNSET
RICKY MARTIN
ALBUM OUT MAY 11
Livin' La Vida Loca
RICKY MARTIN
RICKY
ALBUM OUT

"Livin' la Vida Loca."
©Nina Prommer/Globe Photos

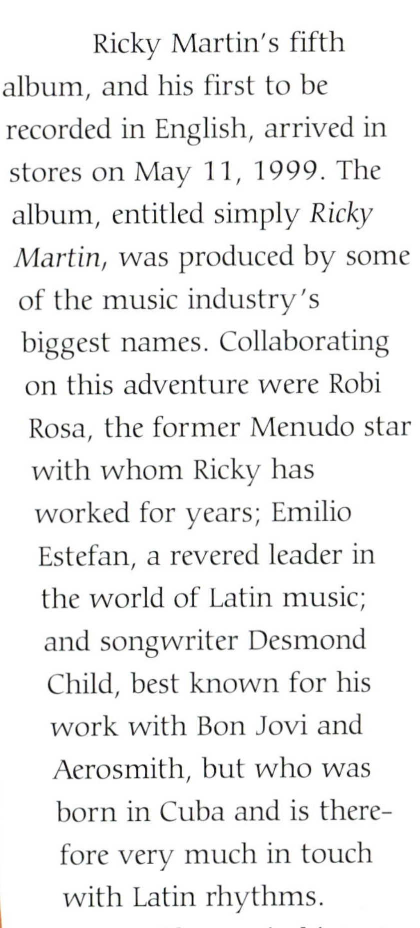

Ricky Martin's fifth album, and his first to be recorded in English, arrived in stores on May 11, 1999. The album, entitled simply *Ricky Martin*, was produced by some of the music industry's biggest names. Collaborating on this adventure were Robi Rosa, the former Menudo star with whom Ricky has worked for years; Emilio Estefan, a revered leader in the world of Latin music; and songwriter Desmond Child, best known for his work with Bon Jovi and Aerosmith, but who was born in Cuba and is therefore very much in touch with Latin rhythms.

The musical intent of *Ricky Martin* was to blend the Latin rhythms that had made Ricky internationally famous with the sounds of American pop music. The underlying intent was for Ricky Martin to reach as many people as possible with his music, to communicate his emotions, not just his rhythms, to a much larger audience. In *Ricky Martin*, technology is overshadowed by emotion. And while Ricky acknowledges that technology can be a great component when it is used well, he also likes to remain true to his style, which is simple. He does not want his voice to have a technical sound to it but rather wants to maintain its purity, something he feels allows the emotion of his songs to better come through. "I don't want my voice to sound too technical. I want it to sound like me. The way I feel is, I don't have to sound perfect, but my emotion has to nail it. There's nothing scientific about it, it's all about emotion. I let it flow. If it's real, it stays."

If the success of the album's first single, "Livin' la Vida Loca," is any indication of how the album will do, *Ricky Martin* will be another chart buster. Released on April 20, "Livin' la Vida Loca" was given immediate play on Top 40 radio stations around the country. The Spanish version of the single, entitled "La Vida Loca," rose to the number one spot on Spanish language radio in the United States within days of its release; "Livin' la Vida Loca" is close behind. And MTV played Ricky's new video to the delight of dancing fans everywhere. This pulsating song combines some rock elements with Latin rhythms and, as Ricky says, "there's even a little bit of the sixties sort of a James Bond sound." However the sound might be described, Ricky Martin's "Livin' la Vida Loca" is heating up airwaves across the country and once again getting people up and on their feet, moving to a beat their bodies just can't refuse.

Ricky Martin also includes several other tracks that

Just a few days after winning his Grammy Award, Ricky wowed the crowd at the "Festival di San Remo" on the Italian Riviera.
©AP Photo/Luca Bruno.

are bound to follow "Livin' la Vida Loca" to the top of the charts. One song destined to mirror the success of the album's first single is the duet that Ricky sings with Madonna. When Madonna "discovered" Martin at the Grammy Awards in February, she immediately expressed her interest in recording a song with the sexy Puerto Rican superstar. Ricky knew that this was an opportunity he could not miss. Whether or not the track ended up on his upcoming album, or whether he just had the experience of working with one of the music industry's greatest stars ever, Ricky knew that it was a unique opportunity; he could not let it slip away. "We didn't want to think about deadlines or why we were doing it. If it works for my album, great. If it winds up on a soundtrack or something else, great. If it's just for us to go into the studio and have fun, great." The outcome of mixing Madonna's more techno sound with Ricky's Latin flavor turned out to be a success and a perfect fit for Ricky's album *Ricky Martin*. The track, entitled "Be Careful (with My Heart)," is sure to be the next big hit off Ricky's latest effort.

There are bound to be many other tracks on *Ricky Martin* that touch fans either sentimentally or physically, making listeners either swoon or jump to their feet and move to the irresistible beats. The song "I Am Made of You" is one of Ricky's favorites, since he feels that it accurately describes his place in his search for spirituality. Ricky performs another duet on the album, this time with Swedish singer Meja. The track, entitled "Private Emotion," is sexy and captivating. On this album, Ricky Martin includes a variety of musical

Ricky after winning a Grammy for Best Latin Pop Performance.
©Pacha/Corbis

sounds and styles without ever betraying the Latin base for which he has become internationally famous.

Ricky's venture into the U.S. market with the release of his first English language album has been met with skepticism by some who see him as a conformist who is sacrificing his culture and his language in order to win over the massive Anglo market. But for Ricky Martin, having the ability and the opportunity to record in another language is an advantage that he knew he would put to use given the chance. Ricky's identity is truly bicultural, and he dominates the English language perfectly. His goal is to reach more and more people through his music, and if recording an album in another language helps him achieve that goal, then he will do it.

What fans, Latino and non-Latino alike, should keep in mind, however, is that Ricky Martin does not intend to stop recording in his native language. In fact, for Ricky, the Spanish language is the most beautiful and the most romantic, and it is best able to convey those feelings that he expresses through his lyrics. But he will not ignore opportunities that allow him to touch the greatest number of people. "I will never abandon the Latino market. I want to sing in Spanish, English, Portuguese and maybe even Italian. I want to continue to open markets, but I will never forget my public."

Ricky Martin also sees his chance to enter the mainstream market as an opportunity to present America and the world with a better image of his native Puerto Rico. He received some criticism for not mentioning his country when he received his Grammy Award for *Vuelve*. The implication was that now that he was succeeding in the

Devoted fans were enthralled by Ricky's appearance outside Tower Records in West Hollywood.
©AP Photo/Reed Saxon.

American market he would abandon his roots forever. But Ricky was quick to defend himself and his homeland. "The day that happens, I quit," he said. The criticism from the Latino community may very well stem from a sense of ownership of their beloved star, a sense of not wanting to share what they feel is rightly theirs, both culturally and linguistically. The opportunity, however, for more people to feel close to Ricky Martin's music and be touched by his lyrics is one that any star would want to explore. Unfortunately, the American market has previously not been very open to welcoming Latino stars across their threshold. The fact that Ricky Martin has crossed over that threshold brings honor and respect to his people, and the chance for Ricky to create the same opportunities for other Latinos who may wish to follow his example.

Desmond Child recognizes the importance of Ricky's success. "Latin stars have been trying to cross over for a long time. . . . Ricky's a prince who's been groomed to be king." And crossing over has been accomplished by only a handful of artists. While Latino singers Luis Miguel and Marc Anthony, for example, have a considerable American audience, they have not broken into the mainstream market. Gloria Estefan represents a true crossover into the mainstream, as does the seductive crooner Julio Iglesias, and many others continue to fight the battle that has been lost by so many, including Jennifer Lopez and Shakira.

Ricky Martin's accomplishments and his early success in the crossover market are paving the way for more Latino stars to follow, and this success is not being underestimated by the music industry. Ricky's exhilarating performance at the Grammy Awards was a turning point for him, personally, and for Latino pop music as well. Ricky's recording companies have not missed this signal. While Ricky's previous albums were released by Sony Music's Latin division, Martin has now joined up with Sony Music (whose CEO is Tommy Mottola) and Columbia Records (whose president is Don Inner). Ricky joked about this rise in status in a recent interview with *Entertainment Weekly*: "I knew they'd come to me someday. After the Grammys it was 'Yo, this is mine!'"

Sony Music and Columbia have not missed the early warning signs, nor have they missed the dramatic increase in Latin music sales in general. They recognize this growth and the sensational impact that Ricky Martin is having on the American market as a "major cultural movement" and are prepared to take advantage of it by capitalizing on the Ricky mania that has struck the United States. Tommy Mottola recently expressed to *Time* magazine his faith in what he sees as the next big wave to hit the U.S. market. "I have no crystal ball, but my gut tells me that Latin music can be the next big reservoir for mainstream superstars."

With Ricky Martin's Latin rhythms being played across the airwaves on Top 40 radio and his picture appearing in magazines across the world, Ricky has found a new audience. There is a new energy and a new passion for his music, Latin pop music, which has now been recognized not only by the recording companies but by mainstream singers themselves, like Madonna and Will Smith, and by the mainstream public.

Ricky strums his guitar. April 1, 1995, Los Angeles, CA.

VII

Ricky Offstage

Since Ricky Martin's debut with Menudo in 1984, he has lived his life in the world's spotlight—a life of travel, performing to large enthusiastic crowds and being scrutinized by media attention. His hectic schedule and the public adoration this sexy superstar receives wherever he goes are a part of his public life; that is the Ricky Martin that the print media wants to write about, that radio stations want to play and that television programs want to feature and talk about. But there exists another side of Ricky that most adoring fans do not have the chance to see—Ricky the nonperformer. The Ricky Martin that reveals his deepest feelings and emotions very publicly, through his songs, and who gyrates on stage, spellbinding millions of admirers around the world, is quite a different person when the curtain falls.

Ricky brought his dog to a photo shoot in 1995 in L.A.
©Corbis/Neal Preston

This very public and seemingly accessible star has another side, a side that allows him, perhaps, to be who he is when he takes the stage in front of thousands of fans. While not on stage performing and inviting the world to sing along with his romantic ballads or dance to the Latin rhythms of other songs, Ricky Martin is a quite private, even timid, person. Contrary to his expressiveness on stage, Ricky is more guarded in his personal life. "I'm very intimate and it's very hard for me to express my feelings in my private life. I hold everything in; even when I know this could hurt me. I feel I am such an introvert that I need the stage to rid myself of my insecurities, and there I become Superman." The stage, for Ricky, is an outlet, a forum where he can share those feelings and emotions that he does not readily express in his personal life.

When not performing, Ricky is shy, serene and down to earth. He does not strive, as he does on stage, for the attention and adoration he gets when he is performing. In fact, he seems to make an attempt to escape from them. Well aware of his superstar status, Ricky Martin chooses to lead a personal life that provides him with the opportunity to flee the temporary insanity of adoring mobs of fans and the flashbulb frenzy that precedes and follows his every performance, regardless of where it might be. He is a man who has maintained a very tight circle of family and friends throughout his life. And to those few who are privileged enough to break into that close circle, Ricky is a dedicated and loyal friend. He is a private man who confesses that he needs his space in order to find himself again and to center himself. For him, having enough space is a highly valued aspect of his personal life.

Ricky tries to keep his personal life private, but in 1995 he posed with his then girlfriend in Los Angeles.
©Corbis/Neal Preston

Solitude, both before and after his performances, allows him to find himself and to feel focused. Before his performances, Ricky often asks for five minutes alone in his dressing room so that he can hear himself breathe and think, and so he can warm up his voice and stretch. After his performances, Ricky may spend a short while with VIPs before heading to his room, where he rests, reads or dabbles with his computer. These moments spent alone, reflecting and relaxing, are precious to Ricky. He told the magazine *Hola* in a recent interview that he needs to be alone at least twenty minutes each day. This time helps him survive in the frantic show business world. It gives him the strength to keep going, to do on stage what he cannot do off stage—open up, share his emotions. "I protect my space like a temple," Ricky says. This is not due to a paranoia or some type of fear, as some may surmise. It is merely Ricky Martin's way of pulling back a bit, just enough to be able to give more of himself to his fans, enough to show his fans that he is not only talented and sexy but warm, caring and appreciative, too.

Ricky Martin has also turned to spirituality for comfort and to help him maintain his focus and the balance in his life. With a career filled with impressive achievements and one which has made him a worldwide sex symbol, it is understandable that Martin seeks out time to practice meditation and yoga to help keep his feet firmly on the ground. Often just before he goes on stage, including just before his appearance on the Grammy Awards, Martin practices a type of yoga called kriya yoga. In Sanskrit, *kri* means "you can achieve whatever you want" and *ya* means "soul." This form of yoga can be practiced anytime and anywhere, without anyone knowing that you are actually doing it. It is a form of yoga that focuses on connecting your mind with your heart—so that you can actually hear

Ricky Martin brought Rebecca de Alba to the Grammy Awards.
©Pacha/Corbis

your heartbeat and your blood moving through you. It requires enormous concentration and intensity.

Ricky Martin's dedication to finding inner peace is not only manifested in his practicing yoga and meditation, but also in his being a student of Buddhism, going to Nepal to read and meditate, and continually reading spiritual writings that help guide him in his life. Martin is aware that in his career he is surrounded by a great deal of fantasy. He recently told *People en Español*, "You are always looking for applause and for people to tell you 'You're so good!' And you have to be careful because the most important thing is to have your feet on the ground." Ricky Martin keeps his feet on the ground by finding his spirituality and by reading works that help him stay focused on what is important in life. One of Ricky's favorite authors is the spiritual advisor Deepak Chopra, whose book *The Seven Spiritual Laws of Success* serves as a guide to life for him. The message of the book is that by surrounding yourself with the right people and maintaining your focus, you can achieve anything you want. Ricky also enjoys reading anything related to human psychology, and one of his preferred authors is the Uruguayan Mario Benedetti, whose book *La Tregua* is one of Ricky's favorites.

Solitude and spirituality are medicine in Ricky Martin's life. Time spent alone each day, reading, meditating and reflecting, help him stay strong and prevent him from falling victim to the vices of his business. His efforts to grow spiritually and to seek out an existence filled with love and peace insulate him from the all too prevalent evils in the world of show business. By staying in touch with himself and his own spirituality, Ricky Martin is able to conquer hearts around the world as he projects a positive image. He is a balanced and healthy superstar whom fans can be proud of.

Ricky Martin's private nature while not on stage also

extends to his love life. While there does not seem to be a lack of love and romance in Ricky's life, he attempts to maintain his privacy in these matters (as in all other matters) and does not share much with the imploring media and fans. He admits to preferring women who are independent and who express who they are and how they feel. He believes in feminism and is looking for someone intelligent and extroverted who knows exactly what she wants and goes after it. But at the same time he wants a very feminine woman whom he can bring roses and with whom he can be romantic. He cherishes loyalty and honesty in all his relationships, and he expects a person with whom he is involved to be giving, just as he is. He looks forward to the day when he becomes a father, and at this point in his life can see himself with lots of children. He also confesses to having a weakness for women who are Latina, both physically and mentally. He needs a dance partner who can keep up with his Latin rhythms, but he acknowledges that when love hits you you sometimes have no choice, so he does not rule out the possibility of falling in love with a woman who is not Latina.

While the handsome singer does not discuss his relationships, he has been known to date the beautiful Mexican television presenter Rebecca de Alba. Ricky Martin met the beautiful thirty-four-year-old when he was living and working in Mexico in the early nineties, and they have had an apparently on-again, off-again relationship since that time. They were recently seen together in public at the Grammy Awards. Martin, however, is not divulging much. He defines their relationship as one "without compromises or titles" but does seem to indicate that they are, indeed, together. De Alba is currently working in Spain.

For the time being, however, it seems clear that Ricky Martin's focus is on expanding his career and continuing to make inroads in areas previously prohibited to Latino artists.

And whether his future will include his current love interest or not, what is certain is that Ricky Martin will surely find someone who will support and motivate him in his career and who will help him achieve and reach even greater goals.

Also pervasive in Ricky Martin's offstage life is his tremendous sense of discipline and the importance he places on working hard. Along with his spirituality and meditation, it is Ricky's attitude toward life—one that includes a fierce discipline and work ethic—that has allowed him to reach his goals. He realizes that his success has had a direct correlation with how hard he has worked, and he knows that in order to achieve further goals he must press on with even greater courage and determination.

Ricky does not worry much about what others think, but rather focuses on his work patiently and decidedly. Coauthor of the hit song "La Copa de la Vida" Desmond Child marvels at Ricky Martin's tenacity, determined nature and how he strives for perfection. "He deserves everything he has because he has sacrificed so much," he told *People en Español*. "I have never seen anyone work as hard as he does." Martin's sacrifices seem to be spurred by his desire not to conform and his refusal to be mediocre. He is in a fight to "not be just one more," and that fight is leading him to the top of music charts around the world. And Ricky Martin has already proven, and continues to do so, that he is not just one more. By breaking down long-held stereotypes and conquering new regions of the world with his lyrics, both in English and Spanish, the very introspective and private, yet driven and determined, Ricky Martin is achieving a level of success that is unprecedented and, for most, unattainable.

On April 20, 1999, a crowd of fans estimated at over 3,000 waited for Ricky next to this larger-than-life banner hanging outside a Tower Records store in West Holiywood. He was promoting "Livin' la Vida Loca."
©AP Photo/Reed Saxon.

VIII

Livin' la Vida Loca

With his multiple platinum and gold albums, showstopping performances at the 1998 World Cup Final and at the Grammy Awards in February 1999, and his bold crossover into the English market with the release of his first English language album, Ricky Martin is literally "livin' la vida loca." Gone are the days of struggling to prove his talent; gone are the years of being considered just another pop singer. Ricky Martin today is truly living the life of an international superstar. He has become a highly sought-after celebrity, and he is basking in the fruits of all the hard work that has allowed him to reach this point.

Ricky Martin's hectic life today consists of traveling throughout Asia and Europe, much like recent years on tour, but there is a difference—he now travels by private jet. The jets, usually rented for him by his record company, Sony, have seating for either eight or sixteen passengers and can cost the company up to $1,850 per hour. The convenience of traveling by private jet allows Ricky to visit five cities a week. Such convenience and comfort are easy to get accustomed to, and the Puerto Rican superstar is reportedly thinking of buying his own.

Traveling by private jet has also helped Ricky Martin avoid, to a large degree, the overwhelming crowds that attempt to swarm around him as he arrives in a foreign city. This problem has increased dramatically since his thrilling performance at the Grammy Awards in February. He can't go anywhere without being recognized as that sensual hip-gyrating artist who brought the nation to its feet. And Ricky himself is traveling with an even larger entourage of bodyguards, musicians, public relations staff, a manicurist and even a shoeshine person. At a recent tour date in Santo Domingo, Ricky Martin's entourage was said to have occupied fifty rooms! Fame

Ricky Martin arrived by car for the promotional appearance. Avid fans made it to the car, despite the large truck that blocked the street and the security guards holding them back.

TOWER
SECURITY

seems to have come with a price for Ricky—the great sacrifice of his much loved privacy.

When he does find some time to take a break from his soaring career, he likes to do so at his home in Miami, Florida, surrounded by the beautiful gardens and the tranquility of the ocean. Whether meditating while facing the ocean, feeding the birds or reading a book, here Ricky is able to temporarily disconnect from the world and experience privacy again, something which gives him renewed energy to later go out and face the lights again. "My career forces me to always be on the move and be surrounded by people; when I am at home I enjoy being alone." These are, perhaps, Ricky's rarest and, therefore, most coveted moments.

As if his recording career and touring schedule were not keeping him busy enough, Ricky Martin can now add the category of restaurateur to his résumé. Casa Salsa, a restaurant serving Puerto Rican food and modeled after one of Ricky's favorite restaurants in Puerto Rico, Ajili Mójili, opened to much fanfare in December 1998. Located on Ocean Drive in South Beach, Florida, just steps away from Emilio Estefan's restaurant, Casa Salsa is what Ricky intends to be "like taking a trip to Puerto Rico in the middle of Miami." The idea to open a restaurant rose from Ricky's longing for his native Puerto Rico and its food while on the road. When he finally settled in Miami, he decided to get together with a group of other Puerto Rican businessmen to open a restaurant that could be like a home away from home for all Puerto Ricans. Among these men were his good friend and manager, Angelo Medina, and Manuel Benítez, founder of one of Puerto Rico's top gourmet restaurants, Ajili Mójili.

When you enter Casa Salsa, "you feel like you have walked into a modern Puerto Rican house, offering you one of the best cuisines in all of Latin America," Ricky says proudly.

Ricky stepped out and was happy to see the crowd.
©AP Photo/Reed Saxon

In a tribute to Frank Sinatra, Ricky sang "I've Got the World on a String" during the Rainforest Foundation's Ninth Annual Carnegie Hall Benefit Concert. April 1, 1999, in New York City.
©AP/Wide World Photos.

Casa Salsa's menu is typically Puerto Rican and reflects the menu served at Benítez's restaurant in Puerto Rico—traditional Puerto Rican dishes but with an added gourmet touch. The house salsa is the ajili mójili, like the restaurant, and is a secret sauce made from a combination of sixteen ingredients. The restaurant also includes a bar designed after a distillery, an homage to the Puerto Rican rum industry, and there is even a special drink called La copa de la vida after the song Ricky made famous at the World Cup soccer finale. The restaurant also features live music—salsa, naturally. With the opening of Casa Salsa, Ricky has brought yet another element of Puerto Rican culture to the United States, the wonderful tropical flavors and aromas of his country's culinary tradition.

Ricky Martin's life is bound to get even more hectic as the impact of his successful crossover career and latest album continue. He may have even less time to retreat to his home in Miami to "reenergize" if he opts to accept every opportunity that comes his way. His face can now be seen all over magazines and television, and he is being sought after as are only the top stars. In April of 1999, he performed at a fundraiser for the Rainforest Foundation in New York City. At this concert—a tribute to the late, great Frank Sinatra—Ricky Martin sang his version of "I've Got the World on a String." Thanks to the participation of top-billed stars like Ricky Martin, the benefit was able to raise $2 million for the cause. This is just an example of Ricky's new level of recognition, acceptance and influence in the mainstream music industry. Ricky does seem to have the world on a string, and he has only scratched the surface. If he continues to persevere—and he shows no signs of letting up and relaxing with the international fame he has already earned—this ambitious talent's life promises to be even more *loca* than ever.

On October 31, 1998, Ricky Martin poured his heart into his concert at Madison Square Garden in New York City.
©Corbis/Mitch Gerber

IX

The Power of Positive Thinking

Ricky Martin has become one of the world's most coveted performers and in doing so has taken on the serious responsibility of being a role model for his Latin community. He has excelled in a world that has rejected many other Latino performers before him, and he has found his place in the mainstream music industry. Ricky Martin sees his breakthrough success as the result of a coming together of several elements, primary of which is his philosophy that through hard work, you can accomplish whatever you set out to do.

Ricky Martin seems to have had this special gift of positive thinking and perseverance since he left the group Menudo at the age of seventeen. The special training and discipline that Ricky had experienced while touring with the group were the best preparation for beginning a solo career that he could imagine. He believed in his talent and he felt ready to go after—and get—whatever he wanted. Positive thinking proved to be an extremely powerful force, especially when combined with natural talent and charisma. Ricky Martin knew the strength of this combination and used it to take his solo career to the top.

Ricky Martin can also attribute his success to the hard work that he invested along the way. Mere positive thinking and his good looks would not have landed the sexy Puerto Rican a spot performing on the Grammy Awards Ricky worked hard to produce albums that he thought would reach out to his people, albums that he would be able to look back on and be proud of many years later. He knew that in order to achieve fame he would have to work until he sweat, remain positive along the way, and know that no matter how long it might take, it would happen. He never grew discouraged or felt that he had gone as far as he could go. Whatever came his way and no matter how exhausted he was, he stayed positive and kept a smile on his face, refusing to believe that he had peaked or could go no further.

Also instrumental in Ricky's rise to international stardom has been his agent, Angelo Medina. Angelo Medina, who is also a co-owner in Ricky's restaurant, Casa Salsa, is a well-known music promoter and has managed many of the top Latino artists. He was the force behind such Latino singing stars as Emmanuel and Jose Feliciano, and he is

Ricky performing at the San Remo Festival in San Remo, Italy.
©Mark Allan/Globe Photos. 1999.

credited with bringing music sensations Camilio Sesto and Rocío Durcal to America. Medina states proudly, "More than seventy artists have trusted me to guide their professional careers." And Ricky Martin's name can be found on that long list. Ricky refers to Medina as "the angel behind his success," and after receiving his Grammy Award he made a point of mentioning Medina and thanking him for just that, being his angel. Medina was touched by Ricky's gesture but not surprised, since they have had a very special and close relationship for a long time. He points out that Ricky's gesture says a lot about who Ricky is: "a simple and very thankful young man."

Ricky Martin's clean-cut style and image, the messages conveyed through his lyrics, and the high regard he places on his family and friends have made him a star that young and old admire and respect. He has proven to his community and to the world that Latino performers do not need to change their language in order to reach people in faraway lands and touch their hearts, showing that Latino artists do *not* need to compromise who they are or change their form of expressions to achieve worldwide stardom. In reaching other continents with his Latino-inspired rhythms and Spanish lyrics, Ricky can also be credited with bringing the Latino culture, the Spanish language and Latin pop music to people all over the world. He recognizes that his Latin rhythms alone have broken down cultural barriers. After seeing the effect of his music from Finland to Russia to Japan and back to Latin America, he sees that "when that drum hits, it doesn't matter where you're from, you're going to dance. We're all the same, you know."

By successfully bringing his culture and music to foreign lands, Ricky Martin is putting forth a positive image for his country and for people all over Latin America. His mission is simple—to let people everywhere know that Puerto Ricans and all Latinos can achieve the same high goals that non-Latinos have. "My motivation is my people and when I talk about my people, it is all of Latin America. When I talk about Latin America it is a people that for many, many years and many decades were cutting our own wings because we were always hearing that we couldn't do it, we are not able to do it. I just want to go all over the world to let people know that we can do it, that there is talent and hunger for success, that you can count on us." He has taken on this great responsibility happily, since breaking these old stereotypes is key to his success and the future success of other Latino artists. It is also important for Ricky that people understand what his culture is *truly* about, and if he can help change old perceptions then that is just what he will do.

Ricky will continue to promote a positive image for his culture and his people through his music. He looks at his Grammy appearance as a very positive thing for Hispanic culture, to have been highlighted on a non-Latino awards program. His new English language album will also help to prove to non-Latinos as well as to Latinos that a boy from San Juan *can* rise to the level of a world-renowned superstar. Ricky is also helping to better the image of his native country by appearing in television commercials that are promoting tourism in Puerto Rico.

The excitement that this twenty-seven-year-old sex symbol and singing sensation has caused in the music industry worldwide is virtually unprecedented. But Ricky Martin has been in the business long enough to know that in order to maintain that momentum and remain the posi-

In March 1999 Ricky attended the *Vanity Fair* Party on the night of the Academy Awards.

He also attended the Oscar Party at Morton's. March 21, 1999.
©Andrea Renault/Globe Photos.

tive role model that he is today, he must keep his feet firmly on the ground and not let the screaming crowds and the flashbulbs go to his head.

Ricky Martin has put fame in its proper place, which in his life comes after his family, his friends and his spirituality. He knows he has to be careful, since many superstars fall victim to the entrapments of fame and fortune without even knowing that it is happening. Realizing that fame can come to be uncontrollable, he is careful to reflect often on what he has in life and to remember what is really important. "That is why I pray, that is why I need my family and my friends. I find my equilibrium and my balance in them. Money can't buy happiness or friends or love . . . anything that is worthwhile."

Ricky Martin is also aware that by crossing over into the mainstream music world he risks being criticized for betraying his people. But the effect that this accomplishment is having is actually the opposite. The music industry, including music great Tommy Mottola, is taking a closer look at the Hispanic market for new musical talent, and seems willing to invest both energy and money in tapping that long-awaited market. And Ricky Martin is determined to drive his message home that he will never forget who he his or stop singing in his native language. He may now be a mainstream superstar, but he is and will always be Puerto Rican, and he will continue to record music in Spanish, the language that for him best expresses his true emotions and feelings.

The future is bright for this sexy superstar whose talent and experience far surpass his twenty-seven years. He will no doubt continue to cause excitement in the music industry with his future releases, and he may even surprise us by reviving his currently dormant acting career. After leaving his role on *General Hospital* and the completion of his run on Broadway in *Les Misérables*, Ricky Martin left open the possibility that he would one day return to acting. Although he admits that because he started his Broadway career with a show like *Les Misérables* it would be hard to find something that could equal that experience, he says about a return to Broadway, "I won't close off that possibility." As for other possible endeavors for Ricky, he has expressed an interest in someday getting behind the camera and perhaps trying his luck at script writing. One thing is for sure: in thirty years, Ricky Martin will still be in the entertainment world. "I was born for this. I like what I do."

Whatever Ricky Martin chooses to do in the future, we can be sure that he will do it with the conviction, the skill and the utmost professionalism that have characterized all of his prior efforts. He will continue to be a model for his community by presenting the best possible image to his fans. Ricky realizes that he is under the microscope of the public, and therefore he must keep up that image. With Ricky Martin, what you see is what you get. "I don't put a mask on when I get on stage." What he shows his public is how he really is, and that is the substance of which role models are made.

"Ricky is the symbol of the happiness, talent and energy of Puerto Ricans," says Ricky's manager, Angelo Medina. He is even more than this. Ricky's qualities are universal, just like the rhythms and emotions of his music. Ricky Martin has the world at his feet, and the world awaits his next step.

DISCOGRAPHY

©Corbis/Mitch Gerber

ALBUMS

Ricky Martin 1991 Sony Discos, Inc.
Me Amarás 1993 Sony Discos, Inc.
A Medio Vivir 1995 Sony Discos, Inc.
Vuelve 1998 Sony Discos, Inc.
Ricky Martin May 1999 Sony Music/Columbia Records

SINGLES

"Maria" 1996 Columbia Records
"La Copa de la Vida" 1998 Sony Discos Inc.
"Livin' la Vida Loca" April 1999 Sony Music/Columbia Records

Trivia Tidbits

©AP Photo/Reed Saxon.

1. Ricky best describes himself with the word "simple."
2. Ricky defines himself as an artist, not as a singer or an actor.
3. Among the artists that have most inspired Ricky are Julio Iglesias and Miguel Bosé.
4. Ricky loves to read, especially philosophy and poetry.
5. Ricky's favorite book is *La Tregua*, by Mario Benedetti.
6. Ricky wants to be a father someday and have lots of children.
7. Ricky is a sponge when it comes to music—he listens to all types.
8. Ricky's medicine is his family and friends.
9. The quality that Ricky tolerates least of all is hypocrisy.
10. Ricky's favorite designers are Giorgio Armani, Jean Paul Gaultier, Donna Karan and Dolce & Gabbana.

11. Ricky and his mother were blessed by Pope John Paul II in the Vatican in Rome.

12. Ricky is a big fan of Robert DeNiro.

13. Ricky performed on the 1996 Olympic album entitled *Voces Unidas.*

14. Sales of over 6 million for *Vuelve* made Ricky one of the top-selling Latin artists in Europe, Asia and Australia.

15. Ricky Martin has sold more than 13 million albums worldwide.

16. Ricky is a very shy person who needs the stage to really express himself.

17. Ricky's favorite domestic animal is the golden retriever, for their docile and loyal qualities.

18. Ricky's family, friends and spirituality are foremost in his life, even before his career.

19. Ricky values spending time alone.

20. You can join Ricky's fan club in order to receive all the latest news:

Ricky Martin International Fan Club
P.O. Box 13345
Santurce Station
San Juan, Puerto Rico 00908

E-mail: rickym@coqui.net

http://rickymartin.coqui.net

TIMELINE

©Globe Photos

1971

Enrique Martin Morales (Ricky Martin) is born in Hato Rey, Puerto Rico, on December 24.

1979

Ricky Martin, at the age of eight, can already be seen acting in television commercials.

Ricky is already a fan of the two-year-old-group Menudo.

July 10, 1984

Ricky becomes an official member of the teenage pop group Menudo.

July 10, 1984–July 10, 1989

As a member of the popular teen group Menudo, Ricky records, tours and performs for five years.

July 10, 1989

Ricky is rotated out of Menudo and returns to Puerto Rico to finish high school.

1990

Ricky goes to New York City, where he takes some much needed time off. He spends six months there.

1990 (summer)

Ricky goes to Mexico to pursue a career in acting and singing.

September 1990

Ricky lands a role in the theater production *Las Zapatillas Rojas,* which leads to a role in the play *Mi Mamá Ama el Rock.*

1991

Ricky is offered a role on the well-known Mexican soap opera *Alcanzar una Estrella.* He plays the part of Pablo, a musician and singer, a part he will play for two years. The success of the series leads to a spinoff movie entitled *Más que Alcanzar una Estrella.*

1991

Ricky begins his solo singing career, signing with Sony Discos, Inc., in Mexico.

He releases his first solo album, entitled *Ricky Martin.*

1993

Ricky releases his second album, entitled *Me Amarás,* which earns him the *Billboard* Award for the Best New Latin Artist that year.

January 1994

Ricky Martin makes a big move north and accepts a role on American television, in the ABC daytime soap opera *General Hospital.*

1995

Ricky releases his third album, *A Medio Vivir,* and achieves his first real international success. The album eventually goes gold in 1997.

1996

The single "Maria" is released and soars to the top of the charts in Europe.

June 1996

Ricky makes his Broadway debut in the adaptation of Victor Hugo's *Les Misérables.*

1997

Ricky Martin plays a lead role in Disney's animated Spanish language version of *Hercules.*

1998

Ricky Martin reaffirms his status as an international star with the release of his fourth album, *Vuelve.* The album goes gold in July 1998.

July 12, 1998

Ricky performs his theme song for the 1998 World Cup, "La Copa de la Vida," at the final match in Paris.

December 1998

Ricky Martin opens his restaurant, Casa Salsa, in Miami, Florida.

February 24, 1999

Ricky Martin brings the audience to their feet at the Grammy Awards with his performance of "La Copa de la Vida." His *Vuelve* wins the Grammy for Best Latin Pop Performance.

©Pacha/Corbis

April 1999

Ricky's single "Livin' la Vida Loca" is released. It immediately receives widespread radio play on Top 40 stations around the country.

May 1999

Ricky's first English language album, *Ricky Martin*, is released.

1999 (fall)

Ricky tours North America promoting *Ricky Martin*.

NOTES

The following sources were used in the compilation of this book:

People en Español, September 1998
People en Español, May 1999
Entertainment Weekly, April 23, 1999
The New York Times, April 28, 1999
Pocho Magazine, April 30, 1999
Cinemanía, January 1999
Hola, November 5, 1998
Cristina la revista, December 1998
Cristina la revista, February 1999
Cristina la revista, May 1999
Time, March 15, 1999
Latina, October 1997
Soap Opera Weekly, July 2, 1996
People, May 3, 1999
People, May 10, 1999
El Nuevo Diario Interactivo

The following websites and links were also consulted:

www.sonymusic.com
www.rollingstone.com
www.rickymartin.com
www.rickymartinvuelve.com
www.endi.com
www.rediff.com
www.lamusica.com